GLASGOW
IN TRANSITION

First published in Great Britain in 1996 by
Colin Baxter Photography, Grantown-on-Spey, Scotland

Text and Illustrations © Herbert Whone 1996
Foreword © Cordelia Oliver 1996
All Rights Reserved

A CIP catalogue record for this book is available from the British Library

ISBN 0 900455 06 4

Printed in Hong Kong

GLASGOW
IN TRANSITION

PAINTINGS 1958–64
BY HERBERT WHONE

With a Foreword by Cordelia Oliver

Colin Baxter Photography Limited, Grantown-on-Spey, Scotland

Acknowledgements

I would like to thank:

Magnus Magnusson for his article in *The Scotsman; The Scotsman* and *The Herald* newspapers for various art reviews; The *Scottish Field* for use of tram sketches; Emilio Coia for a review of 1962; Johnny Beattie for permission to use his press photo (I have been unable to find the source of Mr Beattie's press photograph and apologise to the copyright owners); All those who have allowed me to visit and photograph my work; The Glasgow Art Gallery and the National Gallery of Modern Art, Edinburgh, for permission to include work in their possession; My sister Muriel Inglis for all her time in tracking down owners of paintings; Nicky Hodgson for her painstaking work in printing many of the photographs.

Herbert Whone's Exhibitions and Published Books

One Man Exhibitions held in Scotland

1957 – Glasgow, McLellan Galleries – 40 portraits
1958 – Glasgow, McLellan Galleries – portraits and Glasgow paintings
1959 – Edinburgh, Aitken Dott Scottish Gallery – Glasgow scenes and
    portraits
1961 – Glasgow, Falcon Theatre – Glasgow scenes
1962 – Glasgow, McLellan Galleries – 40 Glasgow paintings and trees
1963 – Edinburgh, Douglas and Foulis – town and tree paintings
1964 – Glasgow, McLellan Galleries – 40 Glasgow paintings

One Man Exhibitions, post Glasgow

1966 – York, Austen Hayes Gallery – Yorkshire Paintings
1966 – Harrogate, Silver Coin Gallery – The Yorkshire Scene
1968 – Salford Public Art Gallery – Yorkshire Paintings
1968 – Wakefield Public Art Gallery – Yorkshire Paintings
1969 – Accrington Public Art Gallery – The Yorkshire Landscape
1970 – Leeds, The Headrow Gallery – The West Riding Landscape
1971 – York, Austen Hayes Gallery – The West Riding Scene
1973 – Harrogate, Sands Gallery – West Riding Paintings
1983 – Harrogate Public Art gallery – Exhibition of Tree Photographs
1989 – Fountains Hall, Fountains Abbey – Pastels of Fountains Abbey
1995 – Fountains Hall, Fountains Abbey – Pastels of Fountains Abbey

Books published

1972–76 – *The Simplicity of Playing the Violin,*
    – *The Hidden Face of Music,*
    – *The Integrated Violinist,* (Gollancz)
1975 – *The Essential West Riding,* photographs and writing, (Smith
    Settle, Otley), reissued 1987
1977 – *Church Monastery Cathedral,* Church symbolism, (Element
    Books), reissued 1991
1985 – *Nursery Rhymes for Adult Children,* (Skilton)
1987 – *Fountains Abbey,* photographs and documents, (Smith Settle,
    Otley)
1990 – *Touch Wood,* tree photographs and literature, (Smith Settle,
    Otley)

The Colour Plates

Dedicated to my colleagues in the
Scottish National Orchestra:
1955 – 64

Portrait of Paul Kilburn,
Assistant Librarian of the Scottish National Orchestra 1950 – 58.
oil on wood, 1956 – 22" x 18"
(Mr & Mrs H. Walker, Birmingham)

PREFACE

Why an artist is moved to identify with a particular theme, and in what manner he gives expression to it, is one of the mysteries of life. It is clearly to do with the whole network of forces that make up his unique life and being. So it is not my intention to try to unravel why Glasgow made such a deep impression upon me, an outsider, as soon as I put my foot there. It simply did, and I set to work registering it without any ulterior motive than that I was moved to do so. I had not previously visited Glasgow, and certainly had no conscious intention, whilst there, of recording the end of an era – indeed, at the time I do not think I was aware of the enormity of the changes that were due to happen. It was only in retrospect, 25 to 30 years later, when the Glasgow I had known no longer existed, that I realised that this is what I had done – and understood why it is that now the paintings are coming to be regarded, at least, as being of historical interest.

When I arrived in the late 1950s, I was still involved in portraiture, fascinated by human character, but within two years Glasgow had taken over. The images were so numerous and so powerful that I only had time to register a small proportion of what I saw. It has to be remembered that my full-time position in an orchestra (latterly as deputy-leader), though relatively fluid compared to most professions, filled much of my working day. Quick changing to evening dress from painting gear was a common occurrence, and it is a miracle I did not miss the opening bars of any concert or rehearsal. (Even so, to a close observer, the fingers playing a Mozart overture were often short of being immaculately clean.) Also, regrettably, it took two years to arrive at a sureness of technique, especially in regard to colour, and consequently I destroyed much of my early work. The few paintings that exist from that early period tend to have an element of drabness which I later overcame. Strangely, this does not apply in the same degree to the portraits I was doing at the time.

Visiting Glasgow now, after its cleaning up operation, it is hard to recall that, apart from a few months in the summer, Glasgow used to reek in atmosphere – the sunlight always seemed to be filtering through fog, mist or rain. White and wet skies reflected the black buildings on the roads, at every street corner people seemed to be pushing carts or prams, the latter containing either babies or bundles of assorted clothes. Equally ubiquitous were the children's drawings covering the tenement walls, and the trams that grated round corners noisily and unsteadily as though they were about to derail themselves at any moment. It seems platitudinous, but I can only say that Glasgow had character. It was a character I claimed at the time to be reminiscent of Paris, where I had not long before been a student, or of the hard river life of the Volga depicted in Gorky's autobiography. I do not think it was an over-statement. Glaswegians, I came to see, were held together by a long communal tradition centred around the closes where

Children at a Tenement Window, 1958
oil on canvas – approx. 22" x 36"
(owner unknown)

**Mother and Children
at a Window, 1958**
oil on canvas – approx. 16" x 21"
(owner unknown)

Portrait of Sir Adrian Boult, 1957
oil on board – 20" x 12"
(possession of artist)

children played and women stood gossiping, or simply hung out of a window to pass the time of day. The word 'hen', so frequently heard, gave the impression of a password indicating that any problem could be shared, and that it was a history of hard mutual suffering that had tempered this sense of identity and fellowship.

I am not romanticising unreservedly about Glasgow life: returning home late at night from concerts, sights better left to the imagination were all too common, and it is questionable how much certain aspects of Paddy's Market, under the railway arches by the Clyde, and the Barrowlands – 'The Barras' – (now much tidied up) were colourful, and how much they were a legacy of the slums of 100 years ago and later.

But I return to the idea of character. In moving around the city, always by foot or public transport, I felt something vital and earthily genuine in the

**Portrait of the artist's neighbour
in Otago Street, Hillhead, 1957**
oil on canvas – approx. 15" x 12"
(owner unknown)

Portrait of Paul Tortelier, 1959
oil on board – 22" x 16"
(possession of artist)

place; outsider though I was, I felt in touch with what I can only call the living soul of a people. In the first half of my nine years in Glasgow, this feeling was very powerful – it was only later, in the mid '60s, that I became aware of the changes afoot that were undermining this soul. What now is left of it, and in what ways it has been changed, I had better leave to the findings of the sociologists. On a purely visual level, I was of course saddened by the loss of the images that had been the source of my inspiration. Apart from the destruction of buildings, all that characterised Glasgow – tenements, gas lamps, tar-burners, ferries, and especially tramcars – gradually began to disappear from the scene. I could not help but feel personally deprived when I sent sketches in 1962 to the *Scottish Field*

Baby in Pram, 1958
oil on canvas – approx. 23" x 18"
(owner unknown)

Baby in Pram, 1959
oil on canvas – approx. 25" x 18"
(owner unknown)

Pencil sketches done at the foot of tenement stairs

for an article on 'The Last Tram'. It was hard to accept that I would not be able to paint them any more. In addition, on the banks of the Clyde, the sounds from the shipyards were diminishing, and the docks themselves were beginning to fall into disuse.

And yet it is such changes that led, in 1990, to a new Glasgow proudly showing its changed face to the world. Much has been lost, but much gained. Enough has been written on recent artistic and architectural achievements, and the price paid for them in terms of the loss of the old. It is a conflict I do not claim to be able to resolve. It is a condition of this life that no progress is achieved without some negative consequence. This paradox abounds in the world where, for instance, sophisticated machinery destroys individual work satisfaction in manual crafts or where living standards are being raised world-wide at the cost of a boring uniformity. With this conflict in mind then, I will refer to only a few aspects of the Glasgow I knew, as it began its painful transition from the old to the new.

One of my weekly activities was to rise at 6.30 a.m. on Saturdays to catch a tram that would get me to The Barras by 7.00, by which time the traders had already unloaded or were unloading their bundles onto the stalls. The market opened with unfailing regularity, even in the dreariest and most bitter of wintry conditions, and it seemed to me to be one of the hubs of Glasgow communal life. Apart from the social side of it, collectors in those days were still able to make considerable finds, though a collector was not necessarily an educated man or a dealer. I made friends with one or two working Glaswegian men who lived only for this weekly event, and whose homes were crammed with pictures and *objets d'art* found over the years – they were true lovers of art, and would not part with their finds, though living in the most modest of tenement flats. The Barras was a way of life, full of colour and teaming humanity. When I was there, I was always torn between sketching what I saw, simply observing it, or keeping an eye open for an unexpected Goya!

Another memorable aspect of Glasgow was the annual performance of the Messiah on New Year's Day, first in the St Andrew's Hall before it was burned down, and later in other auditoriums. On one particular occasion there was a hard frost with a light covering of snow. I waited impatiently for the late ending of the concert (it was an unexpurgated Messiah), with the idea of rushing off to catch the daylight and doing some sketching near Govan ferry. The air was absolutely still, the sun an unpaintable watery red,

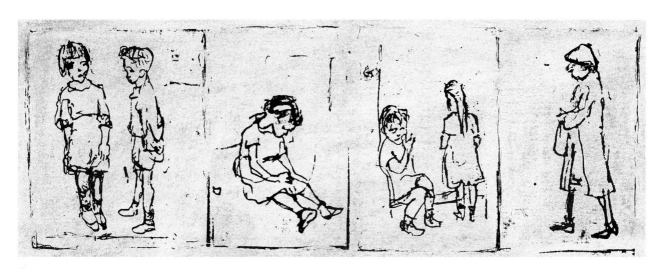

Finnieston Quay showing the dome of the Clyde's pedestrian tunnel
pen and gouache sketch

and the streets were totally empty – not a soul was about. For a reason well known to Glaswegians, it was a deserted city – well, not entirely deserted. Amazingly the ferry at the other side of the river started to make the crossing, and as it did so the strains of a highland melody, sung to the accompaniment of an accordion, and sounding vaguely sozzled, came across the water. There were no passengers – those responsible were the pilot and his stoker. The ferry-boat approached land, and with great difficulty was manoeuvred to the landing stage where it crunched to a halt on the steps. I had to explain then that I had not wished to be taken across, as they had thought.

All experience could not be of that order, of course. Even so, each time I set out to sketch, there was the possibility of something magical – a new dramatic view of a half-demolished building perhaps, or a sudden change in lighting on a wet pavement. Journeys usually started on the midget

**Maryhill Close
Stairway, 1960**
*oil on canvas
– approx. 42" x 24"*
(owner unknown)

underground – a rough and unsophisticated ride, memorable for its strange, though not unpleasant, subterranean smell. They were always planned to incorporate new routes and new territory. One very special and well-worn starting point was through the pedestrian tunnel running under the Clyde at Finnieston Quay. It reeked in atmosphere and was little known or used by Glaswegians at that time. Not far away on the south side of the river was a factory in Plantation Street devoted to making ships' sailing cloth, the toughest and finest canvas an artist could buy. Visits there were an entry into a world of craftsmanship and machinery that belonged to a bygone age. Almost everything had visual interest. The stairways at the entrance to the closes, still with their gas lights, were a fascination to me, as were the coal carts and horses moving slowly about in all weathers. It would be possible to extend these impressions over many pages. I recall them here simply to indicate the impact that Glasgow made upon me, fresh on the scene – an impact so powerful as to be the impetus for five years of compulsive work.

Finally, I would like to mention the fact that the paintings chosen for the book, apart from one or two in my possession, and some whose whereabouts I knew, are ones I have been able to recover after long enquiries and represent perhaps fewer than a third of the large number I did. When the idea of making a representative collection of them was put forward, I did not realise what an arduous task I had undertaken. Having no thought for the future, I had made no record either of owners or of the work itself, so that it is impossible now to say where many of the paintings are. Fortunately I had photographed a few in black and white, and these are included in the black and white section of the book: others had been recorded in colour, but the majority of the paintings have had to be re-discovered and re-photographed. The rest are not far away on unknown walls, or have gone to the far corners of the earth (I am grateful to those people in Canada, Germany and elsewhere who kindly helped by providing negatives for reproduction). The same lack of foresight accounted for the disappearance of most of the small sketches. Again I had photographed a few, but the majority, done on envelopes, fly-leaves of books, and anything handy, had been discarded as irrelevant.

When the owner of a painting used in the book is unknown, it is so indicated. I would be grateful to hear about these and about any others not in this collection so that they may be photographed for possible future use. The actual identification of the places is as accurate as I can remember. More often than not I did not make a note of street names, though I am able to recall the area and each occasion vividly. In a few instances, street names were on the preliminary sketches and these have been indicated for interest.

Coal Cart and Horse in Rain, 1961
oil on canvas – approx. 18" x 24"
(owner unknown)

It goes without saying of course that many of the buildings portrayed are not now standing.

I hope this representative selection of my work, mostly done in the early 1960s, will find a place in the heart of Glaswegians of both that era and the present one – for different reasons. I feel privileged to have recorded some of Glasgow's character of that time, and would like to acknowledge the years spent there among its people, as the most stimulating, both in a visual and human sense, in the whole of my life. Four of my family of five children who were brought up there, and my wife, all regard it with equal affection. I visit Glasgow from time to time, and am pulled backwards and forwards in feeling – backward to the pleasure it afforded me in the 'old days', and forward in admiration for what it has achieved since.

Herbert Whone, 1996

Sketches of tram and ferry at Govan landing stage

FOREWORD

CORDELIA OLIVER

Individuals born with more than one outlet for creativity are blessed and cursed at one and the same time. A child who is gifted both musically and visually is forced by our essentially specialist society to choose a direction and ultimate career at a comparatively early age, and even when, with strength of purpose, he or she succeeds in simultaneously pursuing and developing a second talent, it is almost impossible to avoid being seen as an amateur in that field. And the word 'amateur', although its primary meaning holds no overtones of the second rate or perfunctory, has come sadly down in the world.

Herbert Whone, musician, painter and writer, has suffered all his life from this attitude, this general inability, in the case of so many otherwise intelligent people, to accept many-sided creativity as a natural, if not particularly common, occurrence. Born in Yorkshire into a family which took music very much for granted as a necessary part of living, the young Bert Whone was made to face in that direction from an early age. His mother in particular – a strong-minded woman with a good singing voice who felt that, given the opportunity, she might have sung in opera – pressed him, as he says, into the music mould.

She was fortunate in that her son was genuinely talented, with the violin as his chosen instrument. An important scholarship, the only one in the West Riding in those days, took him to study at the Royal Manchester (now the Royal Northern) College of Music and Manchester University to do a combined degree course. This was delayed through three years' war-time service, and later he spent two years studying in Paris. It was to take up a post in the first violins in the Scottish National Orchestra that he came to Glasgow in 1956. And that is where this story really begins.

As with a normal love affair between one human being and another, this meeting with Glasgow seems to have triggered off the visual element in Herbert Whone's creative make-up to the point where almost

**Women with Bundles of Clothes,
The Barras, 1959**
oil on canvas – approx. 28" x 20"
(owner unknown)

everything he saw in the streets around him became the stuff of one painting after another. In the nine years of his sojourn in Glasgow he succeeded in making a remarkable record of the great industrial city at the very end of an era of half demolished tenements, tramcars and horse-drawn coal carts. These were the days before the Clean Air Act, and the consequent wave of stone-cleaning, helped to restore confidence and to bring about the regeneration that took Glasgow to its eminence as European City of Culture in 1990.

Half a century ago in Yorkshire, the young Whone would borrow his father's camera, conscious even then of the need to compose, 'to put things in place within a framework.' Drawing, too, came naturally although no claims are made for any precocious talent in that respect. Even more important, if neither photographing nor drawing, he was for ever 'registering' visual images, transforming clouds into human features or animals, for instance. 'This was not just incidental: it became a large part of my life. This visual awareness was always with me. Even on obligatory Sunday afternoon walks with my parents, an onerous duty for a child, I was always looking at the trees with their unique characters and incredible shapes ... and now 50 years on I have put together a book on trees, obviously a recovery of the images I absorbed all those years ago.' (This is a collection of the artist's photographs and literature called *Touch Wood*.)

Women Unloading Clothes from a Pram, Paddy's Market, 1959
oil on canvas – approx. 22" x 16"
(owner unknown)

Road scene with tar burner, Maryhill
pencil sketch

Vehicle ferry and passenger ferry at Govan
pen sketch

Women with shawls
pencil sketch

25

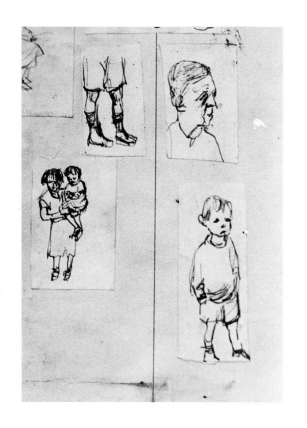

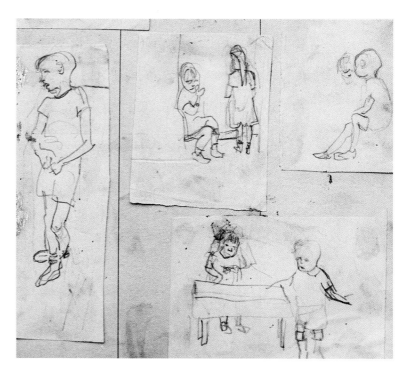

Glasgow children: preparatory sketches

Genuine artists often work in that way, of course: the images themselves may alter superficially, but the motive power remains the same, often going right back to the experiences of childhood. It is interesting, then, that Herbert Whone's most recent work stems from such early roots, and that the link between then and now is photography.

Even before that significant introduction to Glasgow, Herbert Whone had begun to take the painting side of his activity seriously enough to be concerned at his lack of technical training. 'I had been experimenting with portraits of people I knew, learning the hard way through my mistakes – and there were plenty of these. So at the time of my arrival in Glasgow I was just beginning to grasp the problems of painting, having taken nine painstaking years to learn what might have been learnt in two or three at art school.'

The impact of Glasgow on his sensibilities he finds impossible to define, except that it has the same sense as a childhood experience. 'It was as if I and the place were destined to find each other – I was ready for just that stimulus. Almost immediately I had a great compulsion to work – I couldn't wait to get out and find the next image. Everywhere I turned my eyes, subjects were demanding to be caught and pinned down – there was not enough time to record all I saw.' Even his acknowledged lack of technique didn't stop him, although the 'grey patch', as he calls it, of his early days in Glasgow still causes him an occasional pang of remorse when he sees a painting from that blessedly brief period he wishes he could destroy. 'But then things cleared and I started to see in terms of colour; suddenly colour sang out in the middle of the greyness. Glasgow was truly an amazing place to be in – the character of the city, the people, the buildings, the atmosphere: it was something the like of which I had never experienced before.'

The Glasgow of those days had a patina, you might say, of soot, in the blackened tenements, in the drab, working-class areas, and in the winter fogs which were prevalent, as was the case in all the big industrial cities, London certainly not least. And Herbert Whone, with a typically apt phrase, describes himself as '… a dawn-and-dusk person. I like mystery – life is a mystery, not to be found in the exposure to direct sunlight: its fascination is in the corners and in the half-light – things not easily definable.'

So the images Whone found irresistible were those that marked the end of a Glasgow that had its roots in the 19th century and has now gone for ever; images of the trams, clanking along on their rails like genial, top-heavy monsters with tremendous character; street scenes in winter,

Clydebank
pen sketch

bleak as Moscow, with working-class women huddled in the shawls that served them for everything from warm outer wrappings to a means of carrying their infants; dockside scenes with cargo ships tied up to unload. These were the elements around which his paintings were structured with an ever-increasing confidence and skill. But what raised the best of these paintings above the level of ordinary, competent, factual records of place and people was his response to the atmosphere in which everything was enveloped.

A drawing or painting of a tramcar can be accurate and still remain unimpressive. But the same tram, invested with a character immediately recognisable to anyone old enough to remember them on the move, drenched in the damp iridescence of a foggy winter afternoon, the moisture gleaming on the glass – that is the difference between mere

Demolished tenements with figures and prams
pencil sketch

29

Tram under Railway Viaduct
Dumbarton Road, 1960
oil on canvas – approx. 26" x 18"
(owner unknown)

recording of something and the creation of a new 'reality' based on something experienced with more senses than one.

Before long Whone was giving full rein to his compulsion to paint. Before long, too, he had made friends with some of the local artists of his own generation – painters like Tom MacDonald, Bet Low, Carole Gibbons, Bill Crosbie and, not least, Margot Sandeman and Joan Eardley. It was, of course, Eardley who, before she died in 1963, had set her own seal on the image of that declining, disintegrating Glasgow, but hers was an entirely different focus, on the human, and in particular the juvenile, activity rather than on the wider scene. Among the portraits done by Herbert Whone in the late 1950s are small likenesses of his fellow artists, Eardley, Sandeman, MacDonald and Crosbie among them. These are paintings without the usual portrait painter's concern with finesse or flattery, but almost Expressionistic in their search for essentials beneath the surface detail. At the same time an almost painful insight, expressed in forceful brushwork, surely informs the vivid painting of the artist's own

**Tram and Figures,
Cambridge Street, 1958**
oil on canvas – approx. 30" x 20"
(owner unknown)

Sketch from article in the *Scottish Field* on the last tram, September 1962

newborn infant – once again no conventional likeness of babyhood (Plate 64).

But, as to being influenced by Expressionism, as such, Whone can remember nothing of that sort. 'Of course, I was aware of the defined styles and periods of art history, but at the time I had no thought for influences. I now see the relevance of the term "Expressionistic" to my work, but to me at that time, a newborn baby, for instance, was simply a helpless creature – I saw it so and painted it so.'

Because some of Whone's scenes reduce the figures to a totally subsidiary role, they have sometimes seemed reminiscent of the work of Lowry. But this has even less relevance since, at that time, he had never heard of Lowry, let alone seen his paintings. 'I realise, of course, that people might suppose a connection because of the scale of my figures, but though humanly and formally necessary they are essentially incidental to the landscape.'

And, indeed, one can see from the paintings themselves how true that is. The dark-clad women pushing their prams along the wet pavement in London Road are accurately intimated and placed, but none the less incidental to the sombre, towering tenement block against the pale sky (Plate 39). Two distant figures of gossiping women are certainly visible in the top right corner of a small painting in which the main subject is the relationship between a tar-boiler, a huge foreground rain-puddle and the hazy presence of a tenement in the background (Plate 14). What matters here in painter's terms, however, is the importance of even the tiny dark accent made by the two figures in their relationship with the black iron boiler and its broken reflection in the waste of water below.

Likewise, when Whone painted a group of urchins huddled in some game at the foot of a steep, curving, almost medieval stair in Gallowgate, he seems to have seen them very much as an indigenous part of the scene as a whole: the earth reds and yellows of their clothing merging into the drab red sandstone around them (Plate 9). Yet, surprisingly few of these innumerable Glasgow paintings are found to be completely without some sign of human presence. It's as though, for all the excitement he clearly derived from atmospheric quality, the painter realised that, without its people, any Glasgow scene would be incomplete.

So, the stimulus that sent Herbert Whone rushing home to his paints and brushes might well be the sight of the Govan Ferry on a late afternoon in winter, the sun disappearing into a bank of clouds in a fiery afterglow that all but obliterates the ghostly shipyard cranes in the distance, but enlivens the water with roseate splashes and brings into prominence the snow on the riverside roofs (Plate 35). Predictably, however, a second look tells you that the ferry is not deserted: two figures are seen in conversation just aft of its deckhouse.

Yet in the end, the atmosphere is what counts: the blend of visual accuracy and insight. In one painting of two women gossiping in Govan on a wet day, fitful daylight with the shipyard cranes just visible through the mist, a gleam of pale sunlight to the west seems to hold out the promise of better weather tomorrow (Plate 10). Works like these, which had their source in little sketches made in situ, were invariably done as soon as possible after the initial experience. 'Eventually, I arrived at the point where the gap between the act of seeing and its transition onto canvas was almost unbearable. Of course once a thing is known

Shipyard at the mouth of the River Kelvin
pen sketch

intimately, it is no longer necessary to have it in front of one – imagination takes over and vitalises the literal fact.' Not mere representation, after all, but evocation was Whone's concern, and in that area imagination plays a crucial role.

Painting as much as he found himself doing, and becoming conscious of increasing technical competence, Whone began to think of showing his work. From 1958 he held regular exhibitions, mostly in Glasgow, but occasionally also in Edinburgh. 'People kept using the word "compulsive" of me – and in hindsight, I can only agree – my output was enormous, and the only thing needed was the courage to show it all in public. Each time I did so was an educative experience.'

His first exhibition in Glasgow was mainly of portraits of his musician

and artist friends; likenesses in which one critic saw the common distinctive quality as being '... a defensive sadness showing in the intensely individual forms of the human faces.' Certainly these portraits, though far from conventional likenesses, have a power not dissimilar to medieval gothic imagery. They are clearly in the northern European tradition of emotional expression. The painter himself admits that when he first began to make likenesses he found himself unable to see human beings as homogenous. 'I saw people unreconciled in themselves – couldn't see past the division down the centre of the face into right and left – the inner conflicts expressed in that division. I saw the human face, you could say, forged out of such conflicts.'

From then on the bulk of his output was inspired by his experience of Glasgow as it was in that transitional period. His, as we have seen, was the Glasgow of the tall, tottering tramcars in glistening wet weather as often as not; of the broken gable ends of half-demolished tenements with remnants of interior paintwork lending splashes of colour to the grey drabness of the general scene; of gas lamps braving the foggy air and blurred red disks of sun piercing the clouds above the midwinter slush. It was the essence of this east-end and dockside Glasgow scene that Herbert Whone remembers striving so hard and continually to pin down on canvas. This was the subject matter which, drab though it often must have seemed to any eyes but those of the painter in tune with its tertiary hues and subtle diffusion of light, inspired him to discover ever more telling means of colourful expression. Some of the later river scenes, indeed, are positively Turneresque.

Compulsive painter or not, most of this time Herbert Whone continued to earn his living as deputy-leader of the Scottish National Orchestra, a position that affirms his proficiency in the field of music which convention continued to see as his true professional activity, with painting as a hobby to be enjoyed in his spare time. This is something he was long ago resigned to living with. On the one hand, as he says, 'musicians wondered where my real loyalty lay, and on the other, artists tended to think of me as a professional musician who painted: there is justification in this of course. But I did not like the notion of amateur, and often showed my painter friends page upon page of anatomical drawings done over the years – proof I had been a serious student of art.'

There is also the fact that, as a music student in Paris where he first started to paint in oils ('… my first love was Vlaminck because of the power and freedom of his style') he found that in mixing with artists and haunting galleries, the two sides of his nature were even more powerfully reinforced. 'Paris stimulated an awareness of all the arts – and I also began to see their connection with the inner side of human growth, something

Crieff Court,
Anderston Cross
pen sketch

**Snow Scene,
Stobcross, 1961**
*oil on canvas
– approx. 22" x 30"*
(owner unknown)

which I later became very conscious of in my own work, whether it was in painting, writing or performing music.'

Herbert Whone has always been interested in religion, as a student of them all rather than as a devotee of one. 'I have tried to understand the central aim of each one, and realised that behind the formal structures of religions, lies the same message. Their aim is simply to free men from the stranglehold of egotism, so as to let the divine voice speak within. To do this calls for sacrifice – there is no spiritual journey without sacrifice.' It is wrong, he says, for religious sects to make exclusive claims. 'There is only one Truth, and it cannot be defined in normal rational terms – Truth lies beyond the small mind, beyond all dogma and partisan interpretation. The true meaning of the work religion is "to re-bind" or "bind back" (Latin *religere*) that is, to a Source from which the individual soul has become

37

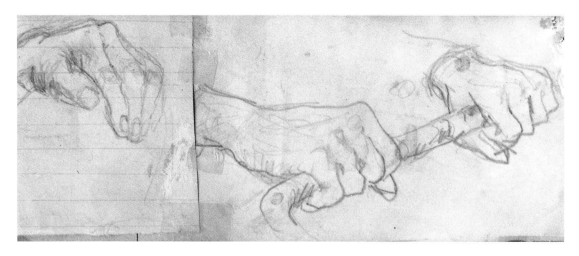

separated. This re-binding can only be achieved by systems that teach how the fallen self may be re-righted – that teach the value of Universal Principles. Despite this dependence on Universals, however, we are all unique. This is very clear in all the creative arts: the principles of balance, rhythm, space, form, control, spontaneity, are identical in painting, poetry, music, ballet and so on, but each artist is a different vehicle. For me, one of the advantages of being a non-specialist has been in keeping a broad horizon in view – in really understanding these principles, and in seeing that we are merely vehicles for their expressions.'

So there is something of the mystic in this painter/musician who could sense as well as see the essential character of Glasgow under its shabby, grimy, tumbledown exterior. This, of course, was something he shared with Joan Eardley whom he got to know fairly well in those last years of her life and whose work he admired, although as he now admits, he was so engaged in his own pursuits that he didn't at the time realise the full extent of her greatness as an artist.

Herbert Whone left Glasgow in 1964, not without much heart-searching, and returned to Yorkshire where he still lives today. His original intention was to concentrate on the painting which seemed to have taken over his life, but, in the end, he decided to continue both pursuits. Abandoning orchestral playing, he taught music, wrote books on the violin, and for a period did radio recitals. At the same time he continued to paint the scene around him, finding a different kind of subdued drama in the Yorkshire landscape; the intrusion of thin, black industrial smoke-stacks in a snow covered countryside, or in the gleam of fitful sunlight reflected in the curve of sluggish canal water under a gaunt cluster of buildings.

'This was obviously the line my life was meant to take – looking at the many facets of the mystery of creation, remembering their unity, and moving as the spirit moved me.' His later work confirms that statement. He has produced a photographic book on the West Riding, a book on Church symbolism, a book of poetry, and a book of photographs and documents on Fountains Abbey in Yorkshire. Also, in 1989 and again in 1995, after a 15-year fast from painting, he held an exhibition of pastels of Fountains Abbey which in terms of texture recall the weather-worn stone of Glasgow. But it is Herbert Whone's book published in 1990 that in a sense takes him back full circle to his childhood, when during walks with his parents, he whiled away the tedium by 'registering' the shapes he saw in nature, in clouds and in trees. *Touch Wood: a Journey among Trees* is a collection of 200 or so of his own photographs, accompanied by poetry and literature on trees, not his own, and often mystical in nature. 'Visually', he says, 'it has given me more satisfaction than anything since that unforgettable meeting with Glasgow 30 years ago.'

Herbert Whone at work on one of his tramcar studies.

A world in swift transition

IT was a stray visit to an art gallery on Saturday that started it all up again — the endless, obsessed contemplation of cities, like Lawrence Durrell worrying the image of Alexandria. For the city is always the most significant agent in our human urban relationships, moulding our character and activities, accenting the whole tone of our living, conditioning our decisions just as illogically as our municipal decisions condition it.

There are so many Glasgows that not even as prolific a writer as Jack House can express them all. It is rich in the ambiguity that pervades all great cities, elusive and contradictory, noble and pathetic, funny and grave, all at the same time. And it is one of these aspects that a Yorkshire musician called Bert Whone has seized and translated to canvas in his one-man exhibition of paintings in the McLellan Galleries in Sauchiehall Street. (See "Unerring eye for drama"—Col. 4).

Whone lives in Glasgow's West End, a fair-haired, quiet young man of 36 who took up painting seriously only some eight years ago. In itself, the West End of Glasgow is a fascinating place, similar in many ways to Edinburgh's New Town quarter.

University mob

As a rough definition, I would measure it as the area within a mile radius of the Curlers tavern in Byres Road. Socially, it has imposing qualifications. Half of the B.B.C. and most of the Scottish National Orchestra—including violinist Bert Whone—live within it. So does the University mob, and lots of artists like Benno Schotz and Ted Odling and David Donaldson and Florence Jamieson and designer Gordon Huntly.

It has the same stone energy of building, now mostly flatted; solid terracings built for more affluent people in more affluent days,' when the shippers liked to be able to look down on the great river that earned them their wealth; a succession of private gardens, which cost the residents a fiver or so a year, entitling them to a private key, which they seldom put to any use.

It's not a particularly bearded area — not Hyndland or Dowanhill or Kelvinside, anyway, although there are fringe growths in the university mazes of Hillhead on the other side of Byres Road. I'm always a little surprised that the university itself doesn't dominate the place more than it does, except for the compelling sound of its quarter-chiming clock. Perhaps it's a reflection of the diffuseness of the university itself—but then, no university on earth could ever dominate fully a city such as Glasgow.

But this is not the world that interests Whone. His source of inspiration is across the river, far away in terms of fashion, over by the cranes that moodily superintend the raucous, swarming tenements of Govan, easily visible from the top flats of these elegant West End terraces,

Street life

This is the world of closes and stairheids, of fecund community life, of old, slippered women going shopping in their shawls, of teeming children, of prams and chalk graffiti on the walls, of real street life where the pavement is the natural arena for debate and gossip and squabbling.

Whone found it rather like Paris, or Rome, full of steepness and stairways and people lounging at the front doors, and much of his painting reflects this preoccupation: sheered-off tenements with a naked gable of wallpapers charting the tastes of generations of forgotten housewives, the lurch and sway and rattle and rumbustiousness of tramcars and the Saturday-night folk who inhabit them.

He is working swiftly to chronicle a world in swift transition, before these vivid children grow up to be shovelled out in the efficient wastes of council housing schemes on the perimeter, before new buildings rise to condition them differently.

They have a fearful energy, these areas, even in decay, an energy that brims and spills into gross inventiveness in coping with the problems of life, a starling perkiness and acquisitiveness and humour. It's a whole civilisation in itself, incomprehensible to Edinburgh; but it's odds on that a lot of the fashionable burghers of Glasgow's West End can trace their own roots to it, and not so very far back at that. And it's typical of Glasgow that they would never dream of denying it.

Magnus Magnusson

Article from *The Scotsman* (above) and accompanying photograph (left)

Railway Arches and Train, Eglinton Street, 1962
oil on canvas – approx. 26" x 18"
(owner unknown)

UNERRING EYE FOR DRAMA

The second one-man exhibition of Herbert Whone, the largely self-taught painter who earns his daily bread as a professional musician—he occupies the second desk in the first violin section of the Scottish National Orchestra—was opened by David A. Donaldson, R.S.A., on Saturday in the McLellan Galleries, Glasgow.

In every artistic way it is unmistakably a considerable improvement on Whone's last show—a judgment so obviously justified that it reflects no credit on one's sense of percipience. The motivation is ostensibly the same Whone is still immersed in drab but evocative Glasgow, the city's shining wet streets over which green cars go east lurching sadly all the way—and not, alas, for long, monolithic tenements standing precariously like old grey sentinels, tar boilers in fog, and coal carts being dragged despondently by dripping wet horses.

All these subjects Whone sees as an expressionist and translates into real painterly terms, each one vividly captured. His eye for creating a picture and rendering the obvious dramatically telling is more often than not unerring, and one only finds him disappointing and in artistic difficulty when he strives for effect and over-emphasis. These are, however, mainly faults of technique, and they are not often obtrusive.

Idiomatic

In this show, Whone has also concentrated on tree forms and tree stumps, and his "Fallen Pine Tree," "Trees In November," and "March Landscape Near Aviemore," are thoroughly idiomatic and in visual character with his chosen landscape.

The pity is that Whone's pictures do not hang well together, and in close proximity one to the other—as they are so displayed — their impact is greatly dissipated.

If Herbert Whone is as accomplished an artist with the bow as he is with the brush then he is indeed well gifted by providence. The exhibition is open daily from 11 a.m. to 6 p.m. until Saturday, May 19.　　**E. C.**

Tar Burners in Fog, 1961
oil on canvas – approx. 26" x 18"
(owner unknown)

GLASGOW SEEN THROUGH FRESH EYES

By Our Art Critic

To be able to paint Glasgow —or, for that matter, any place —as it deserves; to get down beneath the surface detail, however attractive or, to the average eye, dull, it almost seems as though one must see it with a fresh eye.

This is, precisely what Herbert Whone, who came to live here several year ago, is doing.

At his best this painter (the fact that his first profession is that of violinist is really of little interest in this context, for undoubtedly he is a painter of growing stature) is able to take familiar objects of the Glasgow street scene—coal carts, tar boilers, trams, tall tenements, spindly legged children, and everywhere the cast-iron gas lamp—and find in them a strange beauty against the pale yellow evening light or the blinding brilliance of holes in the rain clouds.

Technically, Whone is developing fast and his wet, heavy, loaded brush is becoming much more sure (the fact that, in this exhibition, some 40 of his paintings fill a large room at the McLellan Galleries in Glasgow speaks for itself) so that, increasingly, one sees through the pigment to the essence of his subject.

Perhaps his failures are more obvious (not more numerous) than those of many a painter who depends more on technical virtuosity, and whose hand will carry him smoothly over less inspired moments, but here one feels that, every time, an effort is made to find some fundamental aspect of the subject.

Sketch from article in the *Scottish Field* on the last tram, September 1962

44

HERBERT WHONE

Town and tree studies

By Sydney Goodsir Smith

At Douglas & Foulis, 9 Castle Street, Edinburgh, Herbert Whone is showing 25 "Town and Tree Studies"; the town is Glasgow and the trees are Highland. Herbert Whone is a romantic in love with decaying tenements and red, low-hanging winter suns, mist and fog. In his affection for crumbling wall surfaces, the silhouettes of lamp-posts, chimney-stalks, tall slabs of buildings, trams, coal carts, patient nags and defeated people, he reminds one by turns (or in intermingledom) of Utrillo, Eardley, Lowrie and Morrison.

This artist is at his best in these squalid and depressing surroundings, transmuting, however, the brute-reality (which he reserves for his lightning-stricken trees) into romance and genuine sentiment. The glamour of fog and winter sun enshrouding and ennobling a shipyard or a slum street is often very touching and almost always sympathetic. These scenes are not beautiful in any way; the squalor, the dirt and the despair are there; the beauty and the sentiment that he often conjures is purely in the sympathy that informs his approach and his treatment.

Mr Whone is largely self-taught. He has certainly a natural talent and though occasionally crude in execution his sensitivity to atmosphere and climate and his very true eye for dramatic composition and pose give his pictures the immediate attraction of a good stage set or book illustration. I suspect, too, that they might well have more lasting attractions.

From *The Scotsman*, 9 May 1963

COMPULSIVE ART OF ONE MAN

By Our Art Critic

An enormous one-man show by a painter whose output is prodigious and to whom painting is obviously a matter of compulsion. is at the McLellan Galleries. Glasgow, until the end of this week.

If Herbert Whone had selected more rigorously (the largest paintings are all too often the weakest) the exhibition as a whole might have, been more completely satisfying if not more impressive.

Whone is still seeing and painting the Glasgow scene with a sort of large, indulgent sympathy. The two women talking in a gleaming misty morning (No. 49); the tar boiler reflected in an oversize puddle (No. 33); the pile of Indian-red tenements against the slaty sky of a snowy day (No. 41); these, and several others, are as good as anything he has done on this subject.

Docklands

The docklands have increasingly become a subject in themselves, instead of merely a background or, setting, and the best paintings are not those which attempt to grapple bravely with the immense contrasts in scale which close-ups of great ships' hulls always dictate. but the paintings which express an aspect of light and weather.

One remembers a late evening, looking down-river in spent, watery sunlight, where everything seems to dissolve in golden reflections and haze.

There are several vivid studies of a very young baby where the painter, though obviously intensely involved, is completely unsentimental. The smallest of these— for me the best—is seen with a sharp, Gothic intensity, like a detail from a medieval window.

Herbert Whone is an unfashionably unselfconscious painter. Style. one feels, is his least important interest. Perhaps because of this his paintings. in no sense elegant or sophisticated. have probably a wider appeal than most.

Margot Sandeman, Herbert Whone
and Joan Eardley at
the 1958 exhibition in the
McLellan Galleries, Glasgow

A Whone tram on the move –
cutting from a Glasgow evening paper, 1961

COMEDIAN Johnny Beattie
and his fashion model
wife Kitty donned old
clothes today and helped
with their flitting from their
home at 33 Partickhill Road,
Partick, Glasgow.

The artist and his two sons
at the 1962 exhibition in the
McLellan Galleries, Glasgow

THE COLOUR PLATES

PLATE 1

Child with Baby
Merkland Street, Partick, 1961
oil on canvas – 34" x 26"
(Mr Cyril Gerber, Glasgow)

PLATE 2

Tar Burners in November Fog and Sun, 1960
oil on canvas – 7.5" x 4.5"
(the artist)

Tar Burners and Figures,
The Gorbals, 1961
oil sketch on paper – 6" x 7"
(owner unknown)

PLATE 3

Coal Cart in January Frost,
Cowcaddens, 1963
oil on canvas – 26" x 34"
(Mr & Mrs Bernard Keefe, London)

PLATE 4

**Close Entrance with Gas Lamp,
Bridgeton, 1962**
oil on canvas – 42" x 23"
(Mary Baxter, Glasgow)

PLATE 5

Street Scene near Gorbals Cross
with Winter Sun, 1963
oil on canvas – 31" x 39"
(Mrs P. Sandeman, Kent)

PLATE 6

Boat and Cranes at Queen's Dock, 1963
oil on canvas – 50" x 30"
(Mr & Mrs Louis Carus, Worcs.)

54

PLATE 7

Harland and Wolff's Shipyard,
Govan, in Winter, 1962
oil on canvas – 35" x 27.5"
(Prof. & Mrs F. Rimmer, Cambridge)

PLATE 8

Demolition, Weir Street, Paisley Road West, 1961
oil on canvas – 35" x 26.5"
(Janet Hassan, Edinburgh)

PLATE 9

**Close Stairway with Children,
Gallowgate, 1960**
oil on canvas – 42" x 24"
(the artist)

PLATE 10

Women in Conversation, Govan, 1963
oil on canvas – 28" x 22"
(Mr & Mrs J. Fletcher, Fife)

PLATE 11

**Tram with Figures and Wintry Sun,
Kelvinbridge, 1961**
oil on canvas – 28" x 36"
(Eva Maas, Glasgow)

PLATE 12

**Children by a Gas Lamp,
West Portland Street, 1964**
oil on canvas – 30" x 25"
(From a Private Collection)

PLATE 13

Tram in Rain,
Maryhill Road, 1962
oil on canvas – 50" x 30"
(Mr & Mrs P. Haughton,
N. Yorkshire)

PLATE 14

Tar Burners in Rain (undated)
oil on canvas – 22" x 20"
(Mr & Mrs G. Inglis, Wisconsin, U.S.A.)

PLATE 15

House End and Cranes, Plantation Street, 1962
oil on canvas – 39" x 42"
(Mr & Mrs J. Wilkinson, Kent)

PLATE 16

Winter Scene, Plantation Street, 1963
oil on canvas – 24" x 36"
(Mr & Mrs K. Wood, Liverpool)

PLATE 17

Tram in Dumbarton Road, 1964
pen and watercolour – 9" x 11.5"
(Katrina Whone, London)

People Boarding a Tram in Rain, 1962
oil sketch on paper
(the artist)

PLATE 18

Tenements in Yellow Sunlight, Govan Road, 1962
oil on canvas – 24" x 26"
(Mr & Mrs J. Inglis, Glasgow)

PLATE 19

Tram crossing Kelvinbridge in Rain, 1961
oil on canvas – 40" x 56"
(the artist)

PLATE 20

Winter Scene with Coal-man, Rotten Row, 1961
oil on canvas – 22" x 35"
(Mr H. Miller, Salisbury)

PLATE 21

Tram and Figures in Fog, Maryhill Road, 1962
oil on canvas – 42" x 38"
(Scottish National Gallery of Modern Art, Edinburgh)

PLATE 22

Tenements and Crane, Finnieston Street, 1963
oil on canvas – 26" x 34"
(the artist)

PLATE 23

Clyde Ferry from Anderston Quay, 1963
oil on canvas – 32" x 40"
(David Warren, London)

PLATE 24

Govan Ferry in Rough Weather, 1963
oil on canvas – approx. 26" x 18"
(owner unknown)

PLATE 25

Winter Scene on the Clyde from Yorkhill Quay, 1964
oil on canvas – approx. 22" x 26"
(owner unknown)

PLATE 26

Whiteinch Ferry in Winter, 1962
oil on canvas – 22" x 50"
(Mr & Mrs P. Haughton, N. Yorkshire)

PLATE 27

Winter Scene with Coal Cart, near George Street, 1964
oil on canvas – 35" x 35"
(Mr & Mrs Louis Carus, Worcs.)

PLATE 28

**Tram and Figures in Rain,
Byres Road, 1961**
oil on canvas – 50" x 30"
(the artist)

76

PLATE 29

Tenements with Washing, 1963
oil on board – 16" x 24"
(the artist)

Demolition, Rotten Row, 1964
oil on canvas – 11.5" x 17.5"
(Mr & Mrs J. Inglis, Glasgow)

PLATE 30

Govan Tenements, undated
oil sketch on paper – 6" x 8"
(owner unknown)

**Stalls opening at
The Barras, 7 a.m., 1961**
oil sketch on paper – 6" x 8"
(the artist)

78

PLATE 31

Hyndland Station Stairway in Winter, 1963
oil on canvas – 26" x 34"
(owner unknown)

PLATE 32

Demolition, Bridgeton, 1964
oil on canvas – 20" x 38"
(Mr & Mrs A. Whone, London)

PLATE 33

**Tenement Close at
Anderston Cross, 1964**
oil on canvas – 59" x 40"
(Glasgow Art Gallery,
Kelvingrove)

PLATE 34

Boats at Anchor,
Queens Dock, 1964
oil on canvas – 59.5" x 40"
(Mr & Mrs A. Hunter,
Glasgow)

PLATE 35

Winter Sunset, Govan Ferry, 1961
oil on canvas – 25" x 20"
(owner unknown)

PLATE 36

**Close Stairway with
Baby in Pram, 1961**
oil on canvas – 42" x 24"
(Mrs Carlene Mair, Milton Keynes)

PLATE 37

Children by a Tenement Wall, 1961
oil on canvas – 24" x 30"
(Richard Lloyd, London)

PLATE 38

House Ends and Cranes, Plantation Street, 1962
oil on canvas – 22" x 26"
(Mr J. Norris, Yorkshire)

PLATE 39

Street Scene in Rain, London Road,
by The Barras, 1961
oil on canvas – 26.5" x 31"
(Mr Alistair Stirling, Glasgow)

PLATE 40

Demolition scene, 1962
oil on canvas – 27" x 21.5"
(Mr & Mrs J. Inglis, Glasgow)

**Tenements and Washing,
Maryhill, 1961**
oil on canvas – 11.5" x 21.5"
(Mr & Mrs A. Martin, Glasgow)

PLATE 41

Demolition, Rotten Row, 1962
oil on canvas – 30" x 46"
(Mr & Mrs N. Swindale, Vancouver, Canada)

PLATE 42

Two Women Talking in Rain, 1964
oil on canvas – 22" x 18"
(Mr Crombie Stirling, Lanarkshire)

PLATE 43

Govan Ferry in a Winter Sunset, 1961
oil on canvas – 23" x 42"
(Mr H. Howard, Lancs)

PLATE 44

Children and Pram by a Tenement, 1962
oil on canvas – approx. 22" x 35"
(owner unknown)

PLATE 45

Woman and Children at a Window, 1959
oil on board – 20" x 25.5"
(owner unknown)

**Child holding Baby
by Tenement, 1961**
oil on canvas – 20" x 25"
(Mr H. Morrison, Glasgow)

PLATE 46

Demolition, Hyndland, 1962
oil on canvas – 14" x 22"
(owner unknown)

Close in Snow, Anderston Cross, 1964
oil on canvas – 16" x 12"
(Mr & Mrs W. Angel, Edinburgh)

PLATE 47

Coal Cart with Yellow Sun, Beltane Street, Charing Cross, 1961
oil on canvas – 28.5" x 21"
(Mr Ian Hicks Mudd, Oxfordshire)

PLATE 48

**Street Scene with Coal Cart,
near Charing Cross, 1963**
oil on canvas – 42" x 22"
(Mr & Mrs Gow, Lanark)

**Tenements in Winter,
Maryhill, 1960**
oil on canvas – 44" x 28"
(From a Private Collection)

PLATE 50

Sunset on the Clyde, 1964
oil on canvas – 27.5" x 39"
(Mr & Mrs Ian Gourlay, Glasgow)

PLATE 51

Dock Scene:
Plantation Quay, 1964
oil on canvas – 43" x 30"
(Prof. & Mrs G. Houston,
Glasgow)

PLATE 52

Tenenments by Gas Light, Maryhill, 1963
oil on canvas – 22" x 34"
(owner unknown)

PLATE 53

Demolition, overlooking Dumbarton Road, 1963
oil on canvas – 27" x 35"
(owner unknown)

PLATE 54

Tenements at Cambridge Lane, Cowcaddens, 1962
oil on canvas – approx. 18" x 22"
(owner unknown)

PLATE 55

Tram in Fog,
Maryhill, 1963
oil on canvas – 30" x 18"
(Mr & Mrs R. Jennings,
Stirling)

PLATE 56

Tram in Rain, Maryhill, 1961
oil on canvas – 34" x 26"
(Mr & Mrs Magnus Magnusson, Glasgow)

PLATE 57

**Close Stairway with
Pram and Child, 1963**
oil on canvas – 42" x 23"
(Mr & Mrs S. Sneddon, Sheffield)

PLATE 58

Coal Cart and Horse in Rain, 1962
oil on canvas – 40" x 42"
(Mr & Mrs J. Inglis, Glasgow)

PLATE 59

Collage on board made of parts of a Glasgow
tram destination roll: a gift to the artist's sister,
Muriel Inglis, 1964

PLATE 60

Winter Scene with Figures, Rotten Row, 1960
oil on canvas – 35" x 40"
(Mrs Geraldine Lloyd, London)

PLATE 61

Train on Viaduct in Fog and Snow,
Merkland Street, Partick, 1962
oil on canvas – 35" x 40"
(owner unknown)

PLATE 62

Tenements at Govan, 1961
oil on canvas – 22" x 30"
(owner unknown)

Snow Scene, Stobcross, 1961
oil on canvas – 22" x 30"
(owner unknown)

**Railway Arches and Train
near Eglinton Street, 1962**
oil on canvas – approx. 30" x 36"
(owner unknown)

Ferry and Tenements at Govan, 1961
oil on canvas – approx. 22" x 30"
(owner unknown)

PLATE 64

Baby on a Settee, 1963
oil on canvas – 25" x 21"
(the artist)